Preaching

In

Verse

By

Derek Marshall

British Library Cataloguing in Publication Data.

A catalogue record for this book is available from the British Library

ISBN 978 0 86071 763 8

A Commissioned Publication Printed by

MOORLEYS
Print, Design & Publishing
info@moorleys.co.uk · www.moorleys.co.uk

About the Author

The author likes to tell of his first encounter with the Lord, back in November 1963, when he was taken up into a pulpit of an empty church, with the thought emblazoned on his heart that one day he would become a preacher. It wasn't until after some personal tragedies in his life, and some 49 years later, that he did become a Methodist Local Preacher.

His first reaction was to bemoan all those years he had spent away from the Lord. He was like a man in a hurry, making up for lost time. But then he came to realise that it was those years away from the Lord, his wilderness years, that had actually shaped him into who he was. All the tragedies he had lived through, had changed him, and brought him back to the Lord, a very different man.

Right from the age of 16 years, Derek has found he has been able to write in verse, and in his early years wrote many valentine cards in this way. Inspired now by the Holy Spirit, his verses take on new significance and meaning. No longer a man in a hurry, Derek is content to share his work with fellow seekers.

Acknowledgements

The process of writing this my first book has not proved to be the ordeal I had previously imagined. Most of the content I had already amassed over recent years, so I avoided the situation of writing poems just to fill a book, thus preserving the integrity that each poem had been written to augment a particular service or theme.

I shall always be indebted to the prompting and encouragement I have received from members of many congregations across the Nottingham & Derby District of the Methodist Church. Without you I would not have felt that my poems were worthy of a wider audience, and without you, I would not have set out on this adventure at all.

Foreword by the Rev'd Loraine N Mellor, President of the Methodist Conference

Derek is a qualified accountant who came to my notice approximately seven years ago when we were looking for a new district treasurer. At that time Derek was training to become a local preacher, and he was accredited in 2012. It was obvious very quickly that Derek is a man of great faith and integrity. Over the years Derek has amused us with many humorous poems but there is also a deeply  serious side to some of his work, much of which has been incorporated into his preaching. It has been the responses from his congregations that has prompted Derek to bring these poems together in this, his first book "Preaching in Verse". Whilst it has been set-out as an aid to preachers, covering calls to worship, opening and intercessional prayers, scriptural references and the seasons of the church year, you get a feeling that you are sharing in the author's deep faith and spiritual journey. Some of the verses are both challenging and inspirational and I wish Derek every success in his first venture into publishing. Read and be blessed, challenged and inspired.

Contents:

Why Do We Preach?

Are we preaching just to the converted?
Have we resigned ourselves to that?
Is this why the churches are so deserted?
With dust gathering on the welcome mat.

Is our message today so bland?
For fear of upsetting the few.
Is it not time to make a stand?
By challenging those sitting in the pew.

Am I preaching just for me?
The things I need to hear.
Or am I making others want to see.
The teachings I hold so dear?

In Christ we must keep growing.
Drawing nearer every day.
So, our words we must keep sowing.
And preach a finer way.

There's so much for us to say.
And so much for us to give.
To offer a better way.
To the lives we want to live.

So, Lord please equip me.
When I go out there to preach.
Fill me with your Spirit, but especially.
The people I'm trying to reach.

May my words always strike a chord.
Or reach some inner part.
A new thought explored.
Or some stirring of the heart.

Use me Lord as you may choose.
To preach your word anew.
Help me to make your words enthuse.
And bring glory unto You.

Calls to Worship

As we gather quietly in this place;
Put aside all thoughts of the human race.
Enter God's presence in sombre praise;
In quiet adoration our voices raise.

As we kneel before our God and King;
Our hearts in tune our voices sing.
Speak to us that we might hear;
And let us know that you are near.
Amen.

✠✠✠✠✠✠✠

Lord, we come together in joy and praise.
To bring our prayers and anthems raise.
To seek to hear your inner voice.
To ignite our flame and hearts rejoice.

Let us unite in one accord.
To bring praises to our Heavenly Lord.
Amen.

Let us come before our God and King
In songs of praise let our voices sing.
Let our hearts be open, let our minds be clear.
Let us feel your presence, ever near.
Amen.

Lord we are here, to come and worship you.

Lord we are here, to start our life anew.

Lord we are here, to welcome you into our heart

At this time of worship, we are here, to make a start.

Lord we are here, so that we might closer be

To your wonderful love, and majesty.

Lord so that we know, speak to us clear

And make your presence ever near.

Lord we are here.

Amen.

✠✠✠✠✠✠✠✠

As we come into this Holy Place,

And kneel before your Holy face.

Let our hearts be opened, let our minds be clear,

And may we feel your presence, ever near. Amen

Lord, we seek your blessing on us today.

As we come and worship you.

May your guiding spirit show us the way.

Today, and this whole week through.

Amen.

✠✠✠✠✠✠✠✠

Lord we come before you now,

In reverent praise our heads we bow.

As we kneel before our God and King,

An open heart is all we bring.

Speak to us that we might hear,
And open our ears when you are near.
May this service from its start,
Find in us receptive hearts.
Amen.

We come before you in this place
To praise and worship you.
As recipients of your amazing grace
We start this week anew.
Speak to us so loud and clear
In everything we try to do
And rid our lives of any fear
Today and this whole week through. Amen.

For New Year
Lord, as we welcome in another New Year, let us pause for thought.
And thank you or all the past joy that you have brought.
For all the blessings you have daily given.
And all our actions that you have driven.

May this New Year bring us closer to you.
And may we take your hand this whole year through.
May your love and peace alight our way.
As we walk with you, each and every day. Amen.

Opening Prayers

No words of adoration can adequately describe,
The greatness of your creation we see before our eyes.
The wonder of the seasons and the passing of the year,
Your work is all around us, we see it loud and clear.

You put it all together in a careful loving plan
You saw that it was good, and you handed it to man
The birds and the animals, and every living thing
So great is your creation, we can only marvel and sing.

No words of adoration can adequately repay
The gift of love you share with us each day.
A love that transforms even the poorest heart
And opens the way, for a new life to start.

We speak to you in adoration, but on our knees we must confess
The sins of mortal man we need to re-address.
We know we are not worthy, we know we get it wrong
We know we should try harder and try to get along.

It's hard to take the path that stands out from the crowd.
To be a voice of reason in a world that is so loud.
To live a life so pure, the way that it should be
Is sometimes an aspiration and not a reality.

Accept our confessions as we kneel before you now
In sincere un-worthiness before you we will bow.
Lift off this mantle of guilt and set our hearts free
And make us into the people, that you want us to be.

Forgive our sinful nature, forgive our thoughtless mind
Forgive our selfish attitude, which makes us so unkind.
Forgive us Lord we pray, for the things we did not do
For the love we did not share, as you have taught us too.

Forgive us for thinking that we could manage on our own
When our strength should come from you, and you alone.
Forgive us for the days when we simply weren't our best
So, show us what we have to do, to pass the final test.

Father we have your assurance of forgiveness, that you gave us through your Son
For those who do believe in him, will see his kingdom come.
Help us Lord to be more like you, in everything we say and do.
Take our hands to walk with you, today, this week and our whole life through. Amen.

Lord we come into your presence, our voices raise.
In prayer we offer to you our thanks and praise.
In adoration we come before you now.
In sincere humility our heads we bow.

We know we fall short of the standards you have set.
And we enter your presence with shame and regret.
For all the things, we did not do.
Which would have brought glory to you.

We find it hard to put selfish things behind.
To the needs of others, we are so often blind.
It is sometimes easier to look the other way.
When getting involved, there's a price to pay.

Forgive us for our failure to respond as we should.
Forgive us for not being the people we could.
Forgive us for not putting you first in our day.
Forgive us for the time life leads us astray.

Jesus said we can be free of sin
If we would just believe in Him.
With that assurance we are set free
To be the people, you want us to be.

Lord, help us to journey every day with you.
To seek your presence our whole day through.
May you take and lead us by the hand.
As we journey to your promised land. Amen.

Father we come before you, in adoration and praise.
And we shall acknowledge your glory, all of our days.
We come humbly now, before your throne of grace.
Knowing that we can never earn, your warm embrace.

We come before you as our Father and our friend.
Our comforter and councillor on whom we depend.
We come before you now, because you told us that we could.
To share our concerns, you told us that we should.

As we acknowledge the greatness of your love.
And the blessings that flow from heaven above.
We know, that too often, we fall short of your glory.
And fail to live up, to the essence of Christ's story.

We fail to live our lives, in the way that He taught.
And so often our lives, seem to come to nought.
Forgive us dear Father, for thinking we could manage on our own.
When our strength should come from you, and you alone.

Help us to find that inner peace, by walking each day with you.
Taking our hands, and guiding our steps, this whole life through.
And may every word that we speak, and every action that we take.
Be done in love, for Jesus' sake. Amen.

Forgive Me

Please forgive me, for those things I left undone.
For the times I failed to do, what Jesus would have done.
For the times I looked away, saying it wasn't my concern.
And for all those loving teachings, that I have failed to learn.

I know it is not easy – you said it would be so.
To love even my enemy, whose face I do not know.
To forgive others, when it's the last thing I want to do.
But in the very doing, draws me O so close to You.

Forgive me for the times, I thought I could manage on my own.
When my strength, should come from you, and you alone.
Give me the strength, to always do, what you would do.
And to put you first, my whole life through. Amen.

Offertory Prayers

We ask you Lord to bless the gifts we bring,
The prayers we speak, and the hymns we sing.
Shape our lives that we may be,
Ever faithful, unto thee. Amen.

✠✠✠✠✠✠✠✠

You gave us the greatest gift of all.
Yet our gifts to you seem inadequate and small.
Bless these gifts and those who give.
And daily bless the lives we live. Amen.

✠✠✠✠✠✠✠✠

Lord help us to acknowledge all that you do.
And all the gifts you bestow each day anew.
Accept these gifts, as a token that we care.
And all that we have, we are grateful to share. Amen.

✠✠✠✠✠✠✠✠

Bless Lord these gifts we bring before you today.
Bless our days, as we journey along the way.
Bless our hearts, that we might see the others pain.
Bless our lives, lived out in Jesus' name. Amen.

Prayers of Intercession

Let us pray to make this world a better place.
to bring peace and calm to a divided race.
May equality and fairness be our theme.
and unconditional love more than just a dream.

Help us to see the others' need
a word of love or a mouth to feed.
To share the gifts that we have been given
to hold nothing back or keep nothing hidden.

We pray for those who have lost all hope,
who struggle through life and find it hard to cope.
We pray for a world which longs to care,
we pray for a world that wants to share.

We pray for our church in every land.
We pray for all hearts to understand.
We pray for a revival and a modern crusade,
for an infusion of the Spirit every heart to invade.

We pray for those who are sick and weak,
Who from their pain relief do seek.
May your healing hands on those find rest,
and all their pain and ills addressed.

Lord help us to be more like you,
in everything we say and do.
To make this world a better place,
to bring love and joy to the human race. Amen.

✚✚✚✚✚✚✚

Teach us how to change the world,
As you meant it to be.
A place to see your love unfurled,
Where everyone is free.

A place where love is O so real,
And no one feels afraid.
Where nothing we would want to steal,
And no one is betrayed.

A place where helping is the norm,
And people want to care.
A place where every life transforms,
Because you are always there.

Show us how to make the change,
We need to make within.
And start our lives to re-arrange,
So that living can begin. Amen.

His Prayer

O God our Heavenly Father, we praise your holy name.

Help us to make your Kingdom on earth our precious aim.

May we always seek to follow you, in everything we do.

To take your hand and walk with you, our whole life through.

Give us Lord the things we need, to journey on the way.

Forgive us for every little misdeed, and for the things we shouldn't say.

Help us to forgive others and let nothing us withhold.

To take our place beside you, in your loving arms enfold. Amen.

Other Prayers

To Live Amazed

Teach us to be amazed each day,
At the wonders you have done.
Your greatness shows in every way,
and shapes who we become.

Open our eyes with joy and love,
to see what's all around.
To count our blessings from above,
for gifts that are abound.

Your love enfolds like angel wings,
that keeps us safe and warm.
You think of all the smallest things,
our guard against the storm.

Your love is well beyond all speech,
that we could ever say.
And yet it is within our reach,
for each and every day.

Such special love that you have shown,
so great beyond compare.
The greatest love forever known,
that you are always there.

May all our praises daily be,
for everything you do.
And may we all our whole life see,
the love that's always You. Amen.

First Prayer of the Day

Lord we ask you to bless this new day ahead.
Bless all our thoughts and the steps that we tread.
Bless all our actions and the people we meet.
Bless our conversations, that they may be sweet.

May our minds be in tune, to the needs all around.
And our hearts be receptive to your inner sound.
Let our aim for this day, to bring joy and a smile.
To help somebody feel, their life is worthwhile.
Amen.

Thank you for today

Thank you, Lord, for the time you shared with me today.
Thank you for the blessings I received along the way.
Thank you for the people you placed upon my path.
For those special moments when I could share a laugh.

Forgive me Lord for the things I didn't do today.
For the help I didn't give, for the words I failed to say.
Help me to improve, to show others that I care.
And show through me, that you are always there.

Bless Lord the people, that you have taught me to care.
All their hopes and needs, I bring before you in this prayer.
Bless and be with them, their whole lives through.
That they may experience the joy, of knowing you.
Amen.

Help Me Lord

Help me Lord to see, the things I need to see.
And the things I need to hear, that will help to set me free.
Help me Lord to say, the things I need to say.
And the things I need to do, each, and every day.

Help me Lord to think, like you would want me too.
And purify my heart, every day, anew.
Help me Lord to know, you're standing next to me.
To make me into the person, that you want me to be. Amen.

Sharing time with the Lord

O for the special time we share.
With you each day in simple prayer.
Those times through each and every day.
When you simply take our cares away.

We pour out to you what's on our mind.
And we thank you when the world is kind.
We ask you to teach us and help us to grow,
And to lift us up when we're feeling low.

We ask you to care for those so dear.
For their special needs, hopes and fears.
That they may someday come to know.
A love that will set their hearts aglow.

Thank you, Lord, for the special time we spend with you.
For that great anticipation, we greet each day anew.
To know that you are listening every moment that we call.
That you're our Lord and Saviour, is the greatest joy of all. Amen.

Blessing

Peace Blessing

Lord show us the path to true contentment where perfect peace resides.

Where worry no longer has a hold, and where love and joy abides.

A life in which we feel secure, a life that's free from stress.

If we can put our trust in You, your peace we will possess. Amen.

The Seasons

Advent

Advent welcomes a new church year
And tells us Christmas is nearly here.
But what does this season really convey
To you and I, in this modern day?

Advent means "coming" or "arrival"
Of the one who ensures our survival.
Double focus on past and times to come
The first and second coming of the anointed one.

Advent is a journey when we can say
That Christ has come and is here today.
When we can look to a future hour
When He will come again in power.

We live now between two great events
And must ensure our times well spent.
To be alert for His return
A time to share and a time to learn.

God will come and set the world to right
On the "day of the Lord" He will come in light.
He will come to take us to Himself
United with Him in Heavenly wealth.

Advent Wreath

O Advent wreath, what do you mean?
When you appear upon our Advent scene.
What is it that you signify?
Your majestic presence dignify?

The wreath it is a circle, with no beginning and no end.
It reminds us of God himself, our ever-ceaseless friend.
Its colour speaks of renewal and the meaning of new life.
Of the hope we have in God, in a world so full of strife.

The candles symbolize God as the ever coming light.
To take away the darkness and set the world to right.
Burning each brighter as we light them one by one.
And slowly the receding darkness has begun.

We call them hope, love, joy and peace
And with them our expectation will increase.
The Christ candle we light on Christmas morn.
To welcome our Saviour Jesus born.

We are each called to be a light to man.
To teach the Gospel when we can.
To radiate our own lives lived out.
To show what the love of Jesus is all about.

If only I was a Man (Reincarnation explained)

The farmer sat by a blazing fire, outside, the first snow of winter had come.

Startled by a tapping, he saw a bird, attracted by the light, perhaps looking for a crumb.

Further out the farmer saw a flock of birds, obviously caught out by the early snow.

He had a large barn where they could shelter, but getting them inside, he did not know.

He switched on all the lights and opened all the doors so wide.

There's food and safety there for you, but how to get you all inside?

He sprinkled seed outside the barn, in the hope that they'd go in.

They ate a little but were still afraid to sample that within.

He thought he'd circle round behind, and herd them through the door.

But that proved to be a flop, and he ended exhausted on the floor.

Sitting there upon the snow, a thought came in his head.

"If only I was a bird", I could speak to them instead.

I could tell them I only want to help, and not to be afraid.

There's food and warmth inside the barn, I was only coming to your aid.

Over two-thousand years earlier, God had had a similar thought.

He needed to get through to man, as he was not acting as he ought.

Over centuries God had spoken through judges, prophets and kings, but God they still ignored.

Something wonderful and drastic needed to be done, so that God's presence could be restored.

If only I was a man, I could show them where they are going wrong.

If only I was a man, I could show them how, with each other, get along.

If only I was a man, I could teach them and make them understand.

That I am a God of love, and could show it to them, first-hand.

God became man in the most-humble of circumstances, born to a peasant girl, in a lowly shed.

Born amongst the animals, and laid in a straw-filled-manger, for his bed.

And so, we have that very first Christmas.

The word became flesh and dwelt among us.

Remembering a New Life in Jesus

Do we remember why there's a Christmas, what it really means;
Why God came down to earth as a baby and set the Christmas scene.
How Jesus led a life so perfect, for everyone to see;
And how He gave His life for one and all, but especially for me.

We sing, love came down at Christmas, we sing carols by the score;
But when Jesus came down at Christmas, He changed our world forever more.
He showed us how to lead our lives, especially who to love;
Our neighbours as ourselves, but first, our God above.

He calls us all to follow Him, in everything we do;
Give up the past and take His hand and start a life anew.
He showed us by His example, what to do and say;
And if we believe in Him, eternal life is ours one day.

Those who already know Him, will know the joy only He can bring;
To know that inner peace and contentment of Jesus as our King.
So renew your life in Jesus, and remember all He has done for you,
Every minute He is with you, He loves you through and through.

New Year

Another year has passed away.
Another chapter is now complete.
We cannot change our yesterday.
But the New Year we can greet.

We can resolve to change our life.
To seek a better road.
To find that peace and still the strife
And lose our heavy load.

We can resolve to walk in love
With everyone we meet
To fix our gaze on God above
And our love upon our street.

It may not be an easy trail
But exciting that I am sure.
With Him to guide we cannot fail
To enjoy peace for evermore.

Let's Make a Difference in 2018

Two-thousand and seventeen has ended, and two-thousand and eighteen's just begun.
And we search to make resolutions, of something we have never done.
Let's resolve to make a difference, no matter how trivial or small.
Let's help another individual, let this be our New Year call.

Let's resolve to do something special, each and every day.
To do it without thinking, let nothing get in our way.
Let's make a difference for another, something to improve their lot.
In every situation, let's give it, our best shot.

Let's turn a scowl into a grin, a tear into a smile.
For anyone in need, let's walk the extra mile.
Let's turn hopelessness into a dream, and a dream into something real.
Let's change another life, and the way that someone feels.

Let's be the eyes, for those who are blind, and the legs for those who cannot walk.
Let's be the best listener in the world, for those who really need to talk.
Let's be the friend, to those who are living on their own.
And bring joy into their lives, so they no longer feel alone.

If you are looking for a resolution, now that the New Year's here.

Then trying to make a difference, would be a good idea.

It's something we can do, and our time we can employ.

Because in the very doing, it will bring us so much joy.

Lent

What should I do, now lent is here?
How should I mark it again this year?
Is it a sacrifice to make, or do something new each day?
Can it be something to point me to, a better way?

When I think of His journey from wilderness to cross.
Anything I try seems inadequate, compared to His loss.
What are my motives, what is my aim?
Is it a feeble attempt to share in His pain?

Whatever I decide, whatever I do.
Seems but a pittance, when I compare it to you.
When I think of the sacrifice, that you made for me
I need to do something, because you set me free.

May this Lenten journey have some meaning this year,
May it lead me to new insights, may it lead me to share.
May it lead me to respond with action and love.
And to set my sights clearly on Jesus above.

Ash Wednesday

Remember that you are dust, and to dust, you shall return.
And it is through our penitence and reconciliation that we learn.
With this sign, we mark the beginning of our journey through Lent.
A time for self-examination, for self-denial, and a time to repent.

May we on this journey, examine our inner-self.
May our thoughts be turned towards His Heavenly wealth.
May our hearts be cleansed, may our spirit be refreshed.
And may we live our lives, truly blessed.

Life's Journey

You have shown me Lord, the good things and bad.
You have led me on a journey that started so sad.
You took me into places, I would never think to be.
Another world, another life, you opened up to me.

When my self-esteem had sunk so low.
You showed me Lord, a new way to go.
Sometimes two steps forward, then one step back.
I started to get my life on track.

Am I trying to put past wrongs to right?
As I journey from the dark to the light.
Is my motivation all about me?
To forget the past and set me free.

Each day I realise, there's no place to hide.
And I could only change, when I decide.
The choice is mine, it's my decision to take.
This commitment is all mine, that now I make.

Tiny steps are like giant strides each day.
And I will fall and wobble along the way.
My resolve may falter, but my destination's clear.
And bit by bit, I put my life into gear.

Now my eyes are opened, to see what's around.
And my heart's in tune for that inner sound.
I look out with amazement at every turn.
And every step, is a step to learn.

I may never find the perfection I seek.
But I must keep growing week by week.
I can't stand still, there's so much to see.
As my inner energy keeps on driving me.

My goals are moving all the time.
But still I see the finishing line.
My hearts on fire, what joy there be,
That Jesus could save a wretch like me.

On a Journey

I have started on a journey, it's not a dawdle or a race.
It might even take a life time, depending on the pace.
And though I might fall and stumble along the way.
It's a journey I'm committed to, each and every day.

I set out knowing little, much less than I thought I knew.
What the journey would entail, what I might put myself through.
Each small step has been like a giant stride to me.
And the further that I travel, the more that I will see.

The more that I learn, means the more that I will grow.
And the further that I travel, the more seeds that I will sow.
I am starting now to see, what my own eyes never saw.
And my own ears never heard, in the life I lived before.

Though my journey is unique, I know I'm not on my own.
My fellow travellers will help me, and I'll never be alone.
I am showered with every blessing, my heart feels so on fire.
And though this journey may be tough, my feet will never tire.

Although this journey's very long, my destinations very clear.
And though I've still so much to learn, there is nothing that I fear.
I am filled by His Spirit, I am saved by His grace.
And at my destination, I will see my Jesus, face to face.

For Holy Week

Hosanna was their frenzied cry, as they welcomed Him as King.
Yet four days later, it was a totally different song they'd sing.
Crucify Him, became their cry, so fickle was their support.
For Jesus had not turned out to be, the type of King they sought.

The Messiah they wanted, must free them for a start.
But not by any act of war, but freedom in their heart.
He showed us by His living, the way that we should live.
He showed us by His dying, the way we should forgive.

Was Judas Iscariot just a pawn in God's amazing plan?
Could Pilate have prevented the death of this Son of Man?
Was there only one outcome, when God amongst us came?
When Jesus died upon the cross, was there anyone to blame?

The world had lost its way, as it had before the flood.
And a sacrifice was needed, a sacrifice of royal blood.
He took our sins upon Himself, what a price He had to pay?
Brutally beaten, mocked and scorned, it was the only way.

But that is not the story's end, it's only just begun,
On Easter morn new hope rose forth with the rising of the sun.
Death has been defeated, and from our sins we are set free,
As God's unconditional love, comes to reside in you and me.

How many feet have you washed this week?

Jesus did not mean it literally, when He told us to wash one-another's feet.
To go around with towel and bowl and wash the toes of people, that we meet.
Whilst that was the custom and etiquette of Jesus' time.
It is the principle today, that we need to enshrine.

When we become the servant, to those who have a need.
When we act out of love, with a simple helping deed.
When we put the other first or turn the other cheek.
Then that is several feet, that we have washed this week.

When we encourage the depressed and spend time with those alone.
When we become the legs of those, who cannot leave their home.
When we become a light to lives that would otherwise seem so bleak.
Then that's a few more feet that we have washed this week.

Jesus wants us to serve in every way we can.
To bring his love and joy to every fellow man.
It's a pleasure and a joy and we should always seek.
To see how many feet, we can wash this week.

I drove the nails into His hand

It seemed just like any other day – another man was set to die.

And yet this was not just any man – and I began to wonder why.

I've seen hundreds of criminals face this end, their guilt was there to see.

But this man, seemed different somehow, on that day at Calvary.

They said he was a religious fanatic, but I saw no raving to the skies.

I saw only sad compassion, in those piercing, loving eyes.

What had this man done, to deserve this cruel, cruel, death?

And then forgive us all, before he took his final, final, breath.

It's a day I'll not forget, for as long as I shall live.

After everything I'd done to him, he said he did forgive.

It's a day I will remember, but never understand.

For on that day, it was me, who drove the nails in his hand.

Were you there when they crucified my Lord

It was our sins that weighed him down.
For our sins He wore the thorny crown.
Sins so alarming and sins so small.
When Jesus died, He took them all.

Now we can start again, the slate whipped clean.
By His act of love, at that Calvary scene.
So, if someone asks you – Were you there?
Don't just turn away and distantly stare.

But admit and rejoice, without hesitation or care.
Yes – when they crucified my Lord, I WAS there.

Remembered for his doubts

Where was Thomas on that Sunday night?
When the other disciples were gathered in fright.
Did he believe Mary, and was out looking for the Lord?
Or was he just hiding, for fear of the sword?

Whatever the reason, it was Thomas that missed out.
And will forever be remembered, for his moment of doubt.
All because he was missing that day.
Is it really fair, to remember him that way?

Wasn't it Thomas, who said he was prepared to die.
Which doesn't sound like some doubting guy.
Or when Thomas asked Jesus, "how can we know the way".
It was an enquiring Thomas, we witnessed that day.

Thomas had doubts, just like you and me.
But once removed, a revelation did see.
May our doubts make us stronger and give us eyes to see.
And make us into the people, that you want us to be.

On a Road Somewhere

The two set out for home, both dispirited and sad.
And talked freely about the tremendous week they'd had.
Just a week before, they had entered the city to much acclaim.
Now, there was nothing there, to make them want to remain.

Discussing "what ifs" or "what might have been".
A stranger, suddenly appeared, on the scene.
Walking in step, he questioned their distress.
But his real identity, they failed to acquiesce.

They explained to the stranger, the events of the past week.
But they still did not know him, as he started to speak.
He recounted the scriptures, like they'd never heard before.
And as they reached their destination, were still hungry for more.

They invited the stranger, to stay for the night.
Something about him, made their hearts ignite.
As they sat down to eat, the stranger took control.
And quietly slipped into the leadership role.

As he blessed and then broke the bread.
Something clicked inside their head.
And then they saw Jesus, and suddenly everything made sense.
And almost immediately, he was gone from their presence.

It seemed so clear now, the words that he said.
Explaining how the Messiah would rise from the dead.
How had they not known, how had they not seen?
When that stranger had suddenly walked into their scene.

Past weariness now gone, a new energy suddenly found.
With haste it was to Jerusalem, these friends, now were bound.
Such news they had to bring, they couldn't wait there to arrive.
It's the greatest news that we can bring – that Jesus is alive.

Pentecost

My Friend the Holy Spirit

They've called Him by so many names, this friend of mine.
Some of them scary, some undefined.
A helper, an advocate, a counsellor you see.
Just doesn't describe what **He** means to me.

Like any other friendship, it started quite slow,
Shyly, and quietly, and getting to know.
Understanding my friend, it can take a long time,
To accept Him, to trust him, you're then doing fine.

He's hard to describe, to those you don't see,
The wonderful things He is doing for me.
His approach is so subtle, He's like a sixth sense
The way He leads, no pushes me over the fence.

He puts thoughts in my mind, but leaves **me** to decide,
The decisions are mine, and there's no place to hide.
He knows all my weaknesses, my fears and my dreams
He really is a part of me, or so it seems.

I know that I'm not there yet, the place I want to be.
I know there should be more of Him, and so much less of me.
But I know I'm making progress, with the Holy Spirit by my side.
And every day, is like, for me, a roller-coaster ride.

Filled by the Spirit

I am filled by the Spirit, I am changed by the Word.
I am living a new life, and my hearts really stirred.
My eyes are slowly opening, to the things that are around.
And in giving of myself, a new satisfaction I have found.

I am filled by the Spirit, my heart is now on fire.
And each new day presents, a new challenge to aspire.
I am not the man I was, and not the man I want to be.
But the power of the Spirit, has enabled me to see.

I am filled by the Spirit, my eyes are opened wide.
My sins have been forgiven, and there's no place I can hide.
I am striving on a journey, the destinations very clear.
My strength is undiminished, and there's nothing that I fear.

I am filled by the Spirit, my former life's now gone.
And I'm comfortably residing in the place where I belong.
Temptations may befall me, and things can still go wrong.
But the Spirit will be with me and help to make me strong.

I am filled by the Spirit, my heart is not my own.
And one day I will enjoy, the seeds that I have sown.
I am so ever grateful, for all your love and grace.
And looking forward to the day, I meet my Jesus face to face.

Walking in the Spirit of Jesus

When life appear so hard, we can keep a smile upon our face.
Even through all the pain, there's a joy we can embrace.
There's nothing that can stop us, nothing gets in our way.
Because of all the blessings, we're receiving every day.
Why?
Because we are walking in the Spirit of Jesus.
What are we doing?
We are walking in the Spirit of Jesus.

When we see a lost soul, or a hungry mouth to feed.
And without being told, we recognise a need.
When we see a desperate person, whose life has gone askew.
We can take them by the hand, because we know just what to do.
Why?
Because we are walking in the Spirit of Jesus.
What are we doing?
We are walking in the Spirit of Jesus.

When our time is near, and our bodies becoming weak.
When our strength is all but gone, and we find it hard to speak.
When our eyes grow dim, and our life becomes complete.
There's a joy that's still to come, when it's Jesus we shall meet.
Why?
Because we are walking in the Spirit of Jesus.
What are we doing?
We are walking in the Spirit of Jesus.

Songs

(New words to old tunes)

Love Him with all your might (Tune: Diademata)

Love Him with all your might,
Our God Upon his throne.
See how his love our hearts ignite.
And we are his alone.
What greater love than this,
That he should'st die for me
To join with him in heavenly bliss
Through all eternity.

Love him with all your heart,
This God that Jesus showed.
That we may be like him a part,
A blessing he bestowed.
What greater love than this,
That he should'st die for me
To join with him in heavenly bliss
Through all eternity.

Love him and others too,
Our neighbours as our self.
That we may share his blessings new,
Partake of heavenly wealth.
What greater love than this,
That he should'st die for me

To join with him in heavenly bliss
Through all eternity.

Love him with all your strength,
Though weaklings we may be.
O help us go to any length,
To set the captives free.
What greater love than this,
That he should'st die for me
To join with him in heavenly bliss
Through all eternity.

Love him with every breath
This God who set us free.
Who gave us victory over death,
And taught us who to be.
What greater love than this,
That he should'st die for me
To join with him in heavenly bliss
Through all eternity.

Living Amazed (to the tune "London New")

Teach us to be amazed each day,
At the wonders you have done.
Your greatness shows in every way,
and shapes who we become.

Open our eyes with joy and love,
to see what's all around.
To count our blessings from above,
for gifts that are abound.

Your love enfolds like angel wings,
that keeps us safe and warm.
You think of all the smallest things,
our guard against the storm.

Your love is well beyond all speech,
that we could ever say.
And yet it is within our reach,
for each and every day.

Such special love that you have shown,
so great beyond compare.
The greatest love forever known,
that you are always there.

May all our praises daily be,
for everything you do.
And may we all our whole life see,
the love that's always You.

Themes

Remembering His Creation Plan

We need to remember and question every day.
Those wonders of creation we see on our way.
Those marvellous things that we just come to expect;
Take for-granted, misuse and show no respect.

Have we ever stopped to think of God's wonderful plan;
How He put it all together and handed it to man.
Not a thing out of place, and a place for every part;
So perfect, so marvellous, so inspired from the start.

Do we really stop to think, when we throw out our waste;
When we misuse those natural resources in our constant haste.
That God gave those with love, in His careful loving scheme;
To cherish and to honour God's great creation scene.

We really should remember God's great creation plan;
He made the birds, the animals, then He made man.
Man in His own image, He gave him his own free will too;
To choose to sin or not to sin, or live a life anew.

God gave us all choices, only we can decide;
Whether to face up to the truth, or literally hide.
To accept Jesus as our Saviour, our teacher and our friend;
Is to accept a life filled with love, and a life without end.

Looking through the eyes of Jesus

If we could see what Jesus saw,
would our world remain the same?
Would it change our lives for ever more
and ignite our internal flame?

What we see is governed by life's ups and downs,
No two people will see it the same way.
Through Jesus' eyes we remove the frowns,
and bring clarity to everyday.

We only see what we want to see,
our vision is selective I'm sure.
Whilst Jesus is seeing the real me,
right down to my very core.

He looks at people and sees a need
that others have failed to see.
He recognises a hungry mouth to feed,
and a longing to be free.

He sees the pain of loneliness
we sometimes try to hide.
He sees only togetherness,
In his loving arms abide.

He sees the pleading in people eyes,
when all their hope has gone.
He is a worthy interpreter of sighs,
He knows what's going on.

He looks on life as through the eyes of a child,
where love, simplicity and trust are the key.
On a world where love always reconciles,
and life stops revolving around "me me".

He sees potential everywhere
Not a negative thought resides.
Those hidden depths he is aware,
and so much more besides.

Open our eyes that we might see
the things that Jesus saw.
Open our eyes that we might be,
in a world we can't ignore.

If Jesus knocked upon your door today

If Jesus knocked upon your door today,
would you invite Him inside or send Him away?
Would you keep Him waiting whilst you scurried around,
or pretend you weren't in, and not utter a sound?
Would you go into a panic, not sure what to do,
when Jesus came knocking and looking for you?

Would you pull out the stops for this honoured guest
and present him only with the very best.
Would you pretend to be all excited and glad
when deep down inside you felt ever so bad.
Could you cope with a visit, though not sure what to do,
when Jesus came knocking and looking for you?

Would you be able to carry-on just like before,
if Jesus came knocking upon your door?
Could you continue to be the person you were,
could you ignore the event like it did not occur?
Could you find a welcome, though not sure what to do.
when Jesus came knocking and looking for you.

He wouldn't want a fuss, if He was welcomed inside,
He wouldn't bat an eye, at things you might hide,
He wants to meet you, but just as you are,
through a door that is wide open, and not only ajar.
Could you open that door, though not sure what to do,
when Jesus came knocking and looking for you.

Are you ready to welcome the Lord to your heart?
Where opening the door, is only the start.
Will you let Him come in, to make your heart His home
And accept His assurance, that you will never be alone.
So plan now your welcome, it is so easy to do,
when Jesus comes knocking and looking for you.

Have you met Jesus today?

Did you see Him in that stranger's smile?
Was He the one, that went that extra mile?
That person who helped when all looked lost.
That friend who never thought to count the cost.

Did you see Him in the person, who gave up their seat?
Or that friendly person, walking down our street.
Did you see Him in the man who cleared away the snow?
Or in the person who lifted you up, when you were low.

Although we have eyes, we are so often blind.
And fail to see Jesus, in the faces of the kind.
And what about us – what do others really see?
Do they see the face of Jesus, when they are looking at me?

Love

It is the most mis-used word in history.
It's meaning to many, remains a mystery.
But it's said to make the world go around.
And it's meaning, is really profound.

Song writers and poets wax lyrical to its tune.
And in the movies, there always one coming soon.
In our homes, it's on our television screens.
Yet outside of the hype, we forget what it means.

The Beatles told us, that love is all you need.
Another tells us, it makes your heart bleed.
Sometimes love hurts, and it can change everything.
But what is love? What is its real meaning.

Love always shows itself in an action.
That moves far beyond basic attraction.
It's like showing you really care.
And no matter what, being always there.

It's like never having to count the cost.
When things go wrong and you're feeling lost.
It's like sharing the other's pain.
Without having to try and explain.

It's easy to love those you really care.

But what about the others we're not always aware.

The needy and the hopeless that sometimes we meet.

And the un-lovable people we see in the street.

That is the challenge, that is the real test.

Whether your love measures up, and you're truly blessed.

It's not easy, but you are not on your own.

And when love surrounds you, you are never alone.

What is Love?

What is love – that real love,
That Jesus came to show.
That special gift from God above,
To his creation down below.

It's a love that always see the best,
And keeps going to the end.
It's a love that passes every test,
Where everyone's your friend.

It's a love that never seeks reward,
Or stops to count the cost.
No thought is there for self-applaud,
But to welcome back the lost.

That love can be a special smile,
To everyone we meet.
To go with joy that extra mile,
For people in the street.

No words can adequately describe,
This love that Jesus taught.
A love that brings us all alive,
And without which, we would be nought.

The Bible is always there

When you're feeling in need of wisdom to help you along the way;
When you're unsure what to do, or even what to say;
When life just seems uncertain and you wish someone would care;
The answers right before you, the answers always there.

When you want an insight to inspire you and lift you out of self;
To give you a sense of purpose – a gem of heavenly wealth;
When you need a lifting hand, or a sense of walking on air;
The answers right before you, the answers always there.

When you want to read the old old stories you learned when you
were young;
Of prophets, kings and giants and God's precious only Son.
The stories that touched your heart, like nothing can compare;
The answers right before you, the answers always there.

The answers in the Bible, the answers always there.

Importance of Prayer

I may be getting on, but there's so much that I can do.
To share the love of Jesus, with those without a clue.
To offer a helping hand, and to show someone you care.
To make a call that tells the other, that you are always there.

A welcoming smile can lift the spirits of the lost.
A hug or kiss can melt even the hardness of the frost.
Making others feel welcome, can bring the greatest joy.
To a lonely broken heart, that events have tried destroy.

Above all, we have access to the world's most gracious power.
That brings us peace and comfort, each and every hour.
We have that special privilege, every single day.
To spend some time with God, every time we pray.

Our prayers can help a troubled situation, bring comfort to the sad.
Bring healing to the sick, and encouragement that life is not so bad.
Bring hope when life's uncertain, bring peace when life's a blur.
Bring encouragement when we need it, and be our constant spur.

It doesn't matter if we are aging, and not as fast as we used to be.
We still have so much to offer, I am sure you will agree.
Our prayers are still important, important beyond compare.
For in those conversations, God is always there.

On a Journey

I have started on a journey, it's not a dawdle or a race.
It might even take a life time, depending on the pace.
And though I might fall and stumble along the way.
It's a journey I'm committed to, each and every day.

I set out knowing little, much less than I thought I knew.
What the journey would entail, and what I might put myself through.
Each small step has been like a giant stride to me.
And the further that I travel, the more that I will see.

The more that I learn, means the more that I will grow.
And the further that I travel, the more seeds that I will sow.
I am starting now to see, what my own eyes never saw.
And my own ears never heard, in the life I lived before.

Though my journey is unique, I know that I am not on my own.
My fellow travellers will help me, and I'll never be alone.
I am showered with every blessing my heart feels so on fire.
And though this journey may be tough, my feet will never tire.

Although this journey's very long, my destinations very clear.
And though I've still so much to learn, there is nothing that I fear.
I am filled by His Spirit, I am saved by His grace.
And at my destination, I will see my Jesus face to face.

Based on Scripture

The Rainbow

When I see a rainbow, I know the storm is nearly spent.
And very soon the sun appears, to start its new ascent.
New hope is on the horizon, new joy we can behold.
As the colours of this bow, across the sky unfold.

We know the storm is over, the rainbow is the sign
That God is watching over us, with love that's so divine
There's nothing we should fear, as He watches from on high
And sets His seal before us – His rainbow in the sky.

(Based on Genesis 9:13)

Jacob wrestles with God

All alone by the Jabbock River,
I settled down, my mind a quiver.
I dreamed a very violent dream
As physical as any fight had been.

I was wrestling with a force so strong
But I wouldn't let go, I had to hold on.
Was that my past that I couldn't let go
That always comes back to haunt me so?

At daybreak, I was still clinging on
But I felt my past at last had gone.
If God was teaching me a lesson,
Then he had to give me, His blessing.

He asked me then "what is your name"
And I replied without disgrace or shame.
And because of the struggle that I had driven
A new man was I, a new name I was given.

I have never looked back, from that day I was free.
Because that was the day, that God blessed me.

Eagles Wings

We too can soar on eagle's wings.
To see our blessings from on high.
To face whatever our life brings
To do those things we dared not try.

No longer bound by what we see.
No longer brought low by fear.
From all our burdens, we are free
With our Creator very near.

No lowly grasshopper now are we
Our horizons stretch far and wide
With eyes wide open, it's all to see
When on eagle's wings we ride.

(Based on Isaiah 40: 21-31)

Matthew 5: 20-26

Let not my anger get in the way,
of a closer time with you Lord.
Let it not distract the words I pray,
or make my words a fraud.

Heal the anger in my heart,
let peace reside today.
Then I'm free to make a start
With nothing in the way.

Matthew 5: 43-48

How do we love the one we call the foe?
This fictional person we do not know?
How can we pray for those who treat us bad?
And those wicked people who make us mad.

To forgive and remove a hurt, that's in your heart.
To offer the hand of love, is a simple place to start.
God makes his sun to rise on bad men and good
So let us learn to extend the hand of brotherhood.

Matthew 6: 1-6

Take care to hide the good you do
and keep it to yourself.

Just quietly go your whole life through
with no thought of personal wealth.

Give to those in greater need
that we meet along the way.
Let your heart always take the lead
give no thought of what you pay.

And when we kneel to pray,
do it quietly on our own.
Do it each and every day
for with God we're not alone.

Matthew 6: 16-18

When we fast, do so with joy
don't make it a public thing.
By whatever means that we employ
may we, a deeper message bring.

Matthew 7: 1-5

We see so clearly the others' sin
but never so clear our own.
If only we could see within
then less we would condone.

Matthew 7: 7-12

Help us Lord to distinguish between our wants and our needs.
From what we really want, to the hand that feeds.
Help us to seek the things that are lost
and the things that come with a substantial cost.

If we knock, the door will open.
If we seek, then we will find.
You can make our understanding deepen,
and help us leave the past behind.

Always do unto others
as you would do unto yourself.
Treat everyone as brothers
and enjoy your heavenly wealth.

Matthew 23: 1-12

Listen to what they say, but don't do as they act,
for they parade for all to uphold.
Beware of the admiring glances they attract,
for their love they do withhold.

The master must become the servant now,
and the servant will take his place.
The mighty must their heads to bow,
and each to one embrace.

Let not your knowledge place you apart,
from those who wish to learn.
May your motives come from a tender heart,
and the other becomes your concern.

Matthew 25: 31-46

When we stand in judgement before your throne.
It will be our actions, that we there must own.
For the things we did not do for you.
Will be the focus of our review.

No matter how rich or famous we become.
Or the station in life that we succumb.
It's what we do for others, without a thought.
That will decide, whether we amount to aught.
Jesus said, "what you do for others, you do it for me".
And it's that unconditional love, that sets us free.
"You withhold from me, when you withhold from others.
You are failing me, when you fail your brothers".

When you see someone in need, don't just turn away.
Don't weigh up the costs, or time's outlay.
But just see the need, and what you could do.
And imagine the face of Jesus, looking back at you.

Matthew 25: 40-45

Whose is the face you see
when love you freely spend.
Whose is the face from whom you flee
when a hurt you do not mend.

As you do unto others, you do it for me,
just as surely as I were there.
And when you turn away from who you should be,
you turn away from your Saviour.

Look on the other person's face,
As if it were the Lord.
Seek to embody His Amazing Grace,
and live in one accord.

You do it for Me

When we stand in judgement before your throne.
It will be our actions, that we there must own.
For the things we did not do for you.
Will be the focus of our review.

No matter how rich and famous we have become.
Or the station in life that we succumb.
It's what we do for others, without a thought.
That will decide, whether we amount to aught.

Jesus said, "what you do for others, you do it for me".
And it's that unconditional love, that sets us free.
"You withhold from me, when you withhold from others.
You are failing me, when you fail your brothers".

When you see someone in need, don't just turn away.
Don't weigh up the costs, or time's outlay.
But just see the need, and what you could do.
And imagine the face of Christ, looking back at you.

Luke 5: 6-11

And their nets were full to over-flowing
as they grappled with their haul.
And Peter with his sins all-knowing
at Jesus feet did fall.

Jesus said "do not be afraid"
But "come and follow me".
So they left the life that they had made,
not knowing what the future would be.

Luke 6: 36-38

Help me to listen with unconditional regard,
not to judge, to condemn or to blame'
Stop me being hoist by my own petard
but to care for the others just the same.

Luke 9: 23-24

To follow Jesus is to give up on self,
to think on Him, not o worldly wealth.
To put Him first in all that you do,
and take up His cross and start anew.

Luke 15:10

There is rejoicing up in Heaven like we have never known.
With angels singing praises to our God upon the throne.
When we seek repentance for our sins, its louder they will sing.
Although they cannot know, the joy salvation brings.

John 1:38

What are you looking for?

I thought I knew what I was looking for.
I thought I knew what life had in store.
How could I get it O so wrong.
And my understanding take so long.

We look for security, to have enough,
To get us by when things get tough.
To put things by for a rainy day,
And help us keep our worries at bay.

We look for success, for prestige and power.
To seize the moment, to seize the hour.
To seek others admiration and acclaim,
Can wrongly become life's biggest aim.

Others look for some kind of peace,
Where all our troubles seem to cease.
Where self seems but a distant dream,
And love becomes our constant theme.

I have found what I was looking for.
The thing that makes my life secure.
The purpose and meaning of why I'm here.
Has now at last, become so clear.

John 3:1-16

Nicodemus

I had been as shocked as any, by some of the things he said.
And some of the things he'd done, but still I went ahead.
Much as I tried I couldn't get him off my mind.
So, I decided to meet him, some answers there to find.

I knew I was risking all, to seek him as I did.
So, it was under cover of darkness, that I hid.
I needed to know, "who was this man"?
Where had he come from, and what was his plan.

Learned as I am, I failed then to comprehend.
What it meant by "born again", though I got it in the end.
He talked, and I listened, though not understanding every word.
He talked of love and forgiveness, and something inside me stirred.

The next time I saw him, he was nailed upon a tree.
By then, I had seen the truth he had spoken, and the life he'd
promised me.

John 12:21

We would like to see Jesus

Do we come with anxiety and fear?
Are we embarrassed as we draw near?
Do we know, why we have come?
What has drawn us, to God's only Son?

Did He call us, and we heard His call?
Was it His message, to appeal to all?
Were we just curious, to find out more?
To get the facts and know the score.

Were we drawn by what we had heard?
The pure simplicity of His words.
Were we influenced by what we'd seen?
Such amazing things, what do they mean?

And so, we ask, to see Jesus too.
To change our life and start anew.
To start the transformation of our heart.
Where seeing Jesus, is the place to start.

What is Our Church?

We think of a place full of happiness and joy.
A place of special memories that time cannot cloy.
It's been constant in our lives, it's always been there.
A place for growing and a place to share.

Some of us found God there under its roof.
It's there where some of us learned the truth.
It holds a place in our hearts, that's hard to let go.
But does our memory play tricks of what the facts show?

It's not the building that welcomed you with a smile.
It's not the building when others went the extra mile.
It's not the building that picked you up when you were down.
It's not the building that wiped away the tears and removed your frown.

It's not the building that made you feel loved and warm.
It's not the building that helped make your life transform.
It's not the building itself, but the people inside.
Who gave of themselves, and much more beside.

The Church is the people who meet every week.
Who provide the love and care that we all seek.
The building is not important, we can meet anywhere.
And make new memories, with people who care.

Let's Be Bold

Have we become timid at looking outwards, are we too comfortable
in our own shell?
Not to notice others struggling down the road, who we could help as
well.
Have we lost our very own identity, of whom we were known to be?
Has our compassion been so diluted, that it's now not there to see?

Let's be bolder in our outreach, let's be bolder in what we do.
Let's be bolder in our worship, let's try something really new.

The world cries out for meaning, so what is our reply?
The world cries out for direction, are we still asking why?
The world so needs our story, its truth is there for all.
But we are busy looking inwards, our eyes not on the ball

Let's be bolder in our outreach, let's be bolder in what we do.
Let's be bolder in our worship, let's try something really new.

We have means of communication, our ancestors never dreamed.
We can reach people every-where, our messages can be streamed.
And yet we fail to make new disciples, and to get our story told.
So isn't it time we leave our comfort zone, and do something, really
bold.

Let's be bolder in our outreach, let's be bolder in what we do.
Let's be bolder in our worship, let's try something really new.

There must be more to life than this?

Has the world gone mad? Is it out of control?
Are we spiralling to disaster, down some giant black hole?
Is a time of co-operation, a thing of the past?
Has all integrity gone, or just sinking very fast?

Are things so bad upon the world stage?
That we live in fear of a dictator's rage.
Can the world sink any lower than a nuclear threat?
Is the course of self-destruction already set?

We live in a consumer age that teaches us to 'have more'.
Must have something better than, the people living next door.
Happily getting richer whilst others are so poor.
Do we wear rose tinted glasses, like never before?

Are we any happier with possessions galore?
Is our joy only transient, and drives us for more?
Does our life have any meaning, any purpose at all?
If this is all there is, then life's just a crawl.

There has to be something better, or life's just a waste.
Something very special, to remove this bitter taste.
Something to drive us on, each and every day.
Some absolute reassurance there is a better way.

You will know it when you find it, a life of total bliss.
Then you will truly know, there is so much more to life than this.

Just as we are

Have you heard the good news, has it yet to sink in?
That Jesus wants to know us, wherever we've been.
Whatever our past, whatever we've done this far,
Jesus will accept us, just as we are.

It's not about who we are, or what we think we know.
It's not about what we do, or the places that we go.
It's nothing we can earn, there's no hidden formula,
Jesus will love us, just as we are.

He showed by His actions, the way we should live.
He showed with His own life, our sins did forgive.
For just as He knows, the name of every star,
Jesus is calling us, just as we are.

I am Changed

The more that I learn, the more that I grow.
And the greater my understanding, the more seeds I will sow.
I am a new person, my old life's been rearranged.
I've given my life to Jesus, and now I'm feeling changed.

I have a new confidence, I never had before.
Life's becoming an adventure, I'm trying to explore.
I'm finding true contentment, and my futures been arranged.
I've given my life to Jesus, and everything has changed.

Jesus took me as I was but didn't leave me where He found me.
With subtle changes all the time, and a love that did surround me.
I know I am making progress, and my old life's been exchanged.
Because I gave my life to Jesus, and I know that I am changed.

How He changes me

Am I less blind to the things all around?
Are my ears more in-tune to that inner sound?
Is my life less about me, and more about you?
Does my new inner-confidence tell me what to do?

I may not be where I want to be.
But I'm making progress every day.
Those insights you open up to me.
Bring me joy along the way.

I am not the man I was.
Or the man I want to be.
But I'm a different man, because...
My Jesus is changing me.

He is changing me

Being born again, in reality, is a process and not a one-off event.
Culminating at the very time, your old life's truly spent.
It's a journey of discovery, where loves the simple key.
Because I've given my life to Jesus, and He is changing me.

It's a journey of excitement, the like I've never known.
And I'm doing it with Jesus, so I know I'm not alone.
Every day's a new adventure, my heart is light and free.
Because I've given my life to Jesus, and He is changing me.

It's a never-ending journey, always something new to learn.
Striving to be more like Jesus, and the closeness that you yearn.
I'm not the man I was, nor the man I want to be.
But I've given my life to Jesus, and He is changing me.

Giving Encouragement

Rid me Lord of selfish words and deeds.
Make me receptive to other people's needs.
Let me make it a regular event.
To show another encouragement.

Help me Lord, to focus less on me.
In serving others, help set me free.
Let's say goodbye to time misspent.
And try instead, a bit of encouragement.

I know it's the right thing to do.
To make others the focus of your view.
It will, I know, be time well spent.
To offer up the hand of encouragement.

Help me Lord to put the other first.
In spontaneous actions, un-rehearsed.
Is this not why we were sent?
To be a permanent encouragement.

Realisation

When did it change, when I lost my way?
When the worship of self was the order of the day.
When I was so busy climbing the slippery pole.
I lost all connection with my inner-soul.

I realise now, you were always there.
A little nudge to show you really care.
Such tiny changes, it was hard to know.
When I started to change, when I started to grow.

Self is so very hard to leave behind.
Is more than just a change of mind.
To change from everything I had ever known
Is not something you can do, all on your own.

Step by step, with no disgrace
you led me to a better place.
Bit by bit the veil was gone,
and I truly saw where I belong.

My ambition is to be in your service now,
to work for you as time allows.
My heart's on fire, what joy there be.
That Jesus could save a wretch like me.

Dismissal & Blessing

With a joy in our hearts and praise on our lips.
We go from this place.
With an assurance that God always equips.
We receive His grace.
May the blessing of God sustain us.
May the example of Jesus train us.
May the power of the Holy Spirit remain with us.
Today, this week, and forever more. Amen.